THE PARABLES
OF
JESUS

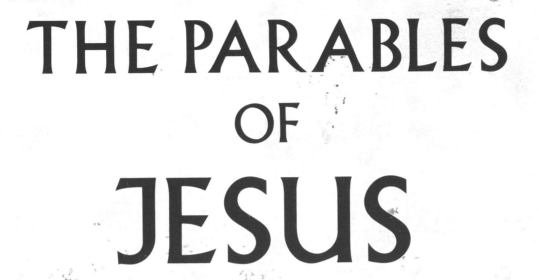

THE PARABLES
OF
JESUS

retold from the Bible and illustrated by

TOMIE dePAOLA

HOLIDAY HOUSE
NEW YORK

For Veronique and the other Sisters
at Red Woods Monastery

Copyright © 1987 by Tomie dePaola
Printed in Mexico

Library of Congress Cataloging-in-Publication Data

De Paola, Tomie.
The parables of Jesus.

Summary: An illustrated retelling of seventeen
parables used by Jesus Christ in his teachings.
Includes "The Good Samaritan," "The Lost Sheep,"
"The Laborers in the Vineyard," and "The Prodigal Son."
1. Jesus Christ—Parables—Juvenile literature.
[1. Jesus Christ—Parables.   2. Parables.   3. Bible
stories—N.T.]   I. Title.
BT376.D4   1987   226'.809505   86-18323
ISBN 0-8234-0636-9
ISBN 0-8234-1196-6 (pbk.)

The parables in this book were adapted from the following New Testament chapters and verses:

THE SOWER   Matthew 13:3–8; Mark 4:3–8; Luke 8:5–8
THE WEEDS AND THE WHEAT   Matthew 13:24–30
THE GOOD SAMARITAN   Luke 10:25–37
THE INSISTENT FRIEND   Luke 11:5–9
THE MUSTARD SEED   Matthew 13:31–32; Mark 4:31–32; Luke 13:19
THE LEAVEN   Matthew 13:33; Luke 13:21
THE HIDDEN TREASURE   Matthew 13:44
THE PEARL OF GREAT PRICE   Matthew 13:45–46
THE NET   Matthew 13:47–49
THE LOST SILVER PIECE   Luke 15:8–10
THE LOST SHEEP   Luke 15:4–7; Matthew 18:12–14
THE UNFORGIVING SERVANT   Matthew 18:23–35
THE LABORERS IN THE VINEYARD   Matthew 20:1–16
THE PRODIGAL SON   Luke 15:11–32; Matthew 21:28–32
THE WISE AND THE FOOLISH VIRGINS   Matthew 25:1–13
THE GREAT FEAST   Luke 14:16–24; Matthew 22:1–14
THE PHARISEE AND THE PUBLICAN   Luke 18:9–14

When Jesus of Nazareth taught his disciples, he often spoke to them in simple stories called parables.

The Sower

Behold, a sower went out to sow.

As he sowed, some of the seed fell upon the footpath, and it was trampled on and the birds of the air came and ate it up.

Some of the seed fell on rocky ground, where there was very little soil.

It sprouted quickly, but when the sun came out, it withered for lack of moisture.

And some of the seed fell among thistles, and the thistles grew up and choked it.

But, some of the seed fell on good ground where it grew and bore fruit a hundred-fold.

The Weeds and the Wheat

The kingdom of heaven is like a man who sowed his field with good seed.

But while the man slept, his enemy came and sowed weeds in with the wheat and then ran away.

When the wheat began to sprout and grow, the weeds could be seen growing among it.

The man's servants went to him and said, "Sir, was it not good seed that you sowed in your field? Where have all the weeds come from?"

"My enemy has done this," replied the man.

"Well," the servants said, "shall we go out and gather up the weeds?"

"No," the man answered. "If you do that, you might pull up the wheat, too. Let the wheat and the weeds grow together until harvesttime. I will order the reapers to gather the weeds first, tie them into bundles and burn them. Then I will tell them to gather the wheat into my barn."

The Good Samaritan

When a lawyer asked Jesus, "Who is my neighbor?", Jesus told this parable.

A man was on his way from Jerusalem to Jericho when he was attacked by robbers, who stole his clothing and money, beat him and left him beside the road half-dead.

Now, a priest came down the same road, but when he saw the man, he crossed to the other side and continued on his way.

A Levite also came down the road and he too crossed to the other side when he saw the man lying there.

But when a Samaritan, who was also traveling the same road, saw the man lying half-dead, he stopped and had pity on him.

The Samaritan went to the man and tended to him. He bound up the man's wounds and bathed them with oil and wine. Then he lifted the man onto his own beast and brought the man to an inn, where the Samaritan looked after him.

The next day, the Samaritan went to the innkeeper and gave him two pieces of silver, saying, "Take care of him and if you spend anymore, I will repay you on my journey back."

Jesus asked the lawyer, "Which of these three men do you think was the true neighbor of the man who fell into the hands of the robbers?"

The lawyer answered, "The Samaritan, the one who was kind to him."

And Jesus said, "Go and do the same yourself."

The Insistent Friend

Jesus asked his disciples, "Which of you knows someone who would go to a friend's house, even though it is midnight, and say, 'Friend, can you lend me three loaves of bread? A friend of mine has just arrived from a long journey, and I have nothing in the house to give him.' "

Now, the man in the house answers from inside, "Don't bother me. It's late and everyone's in bed. I can't get up and give you anything."

But the friend outside is very insistent. He begs and begs and finally the man inside rises and gives him what he asked for.

Even though the man inside would not get up because of friendship, he did get up because of his friend's insistence.

So, I tell you, "Ask and you shall receive. Seek and you shall find. Knock and it will be opened to you."

The Mustard Seed

The kingdom of heaven is like a mustard seed. It is the smallest of all seeds, but a man took it and planted it in his garden and it grew and grew until it became a tree and all the birds in the air came and nested in its branches.

The Leaven

The kingdom of heaven is like leaven, which a woman took and put in three measures of flour and soon it was all leavened.

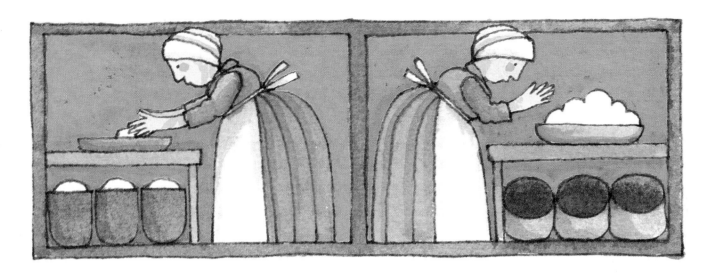

The Hidden Treasure

The kingdom of heaven is like a treasure buried in a field. A farmer finds the treasure. He quickly buries it again and goes and sells all he owns. Then he goes and buys the field where the treasure is buried.

The Pearl of Great Price

The kingdom of heaven is like a merchant who is searching for very fine pearls. He finds one perfect pearl which has great value. So, he goes and sells all he owns to buy this one pearl of great price.

The Net

The kingdom of heaven is like a large net that is cast in the sea, where it gathers all kinds of fish.

When it is full, the fishermen pull it ashore and sort the fish. The good fish, they put in baskets to take away, but the bad fish, they throw away.

So it will be at the end of time. Angels will come and take away the good souls, but the evil ones will be thrown into the fiery furnace where they will weep and gnash their teeth.

The Lost Silver Piece

Once there was a woman who had ten silver pieces, and she lost one of them. She lit her lamp, swept out her house, and looked for it in every corner.

When she found it, she called all her friends and neighbors and said, "Rejoice with me, for I have found the silver piece that I had lost."

In the same way, there is joy among the angels of God over one sinner who repents.

The Lost Sheep

There was a man who had one hundred sheep. One day, one of the sheep became lost, so the man left the ninety-nine sheep and went off to the wilderness to search for the missing one.

When he found it, he carried the lamb home on his shoulders, rejoicing all the way.

Then he called his neighbors to his house, saying, "Come and celebrate with me, for I have found my sheep which was lost."

And in heaven, there will be more joy over one sinner who has repented than ninety-nine righteous people who have no need for repentance.

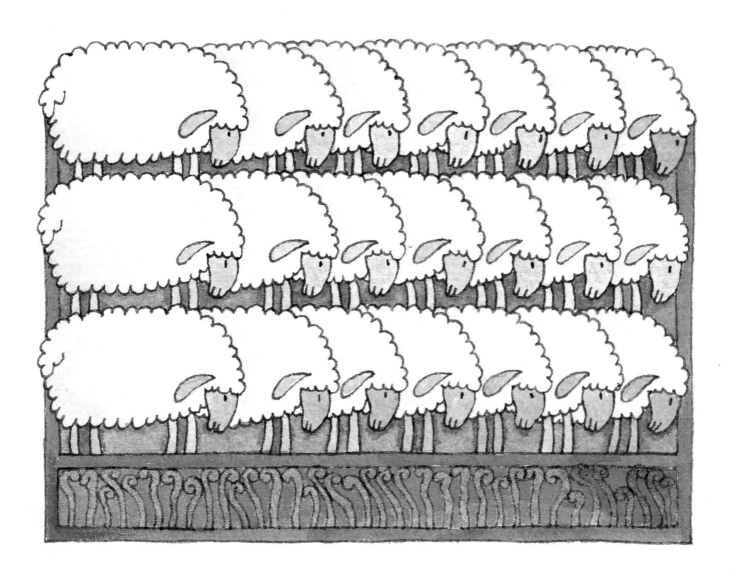

The Unforgiving Servant

Once there was a king who decided to settle all the accounts with his servants.

One of the first men to appear before the king owed ten thousand talents.

He had no way to pay back this large sum. So the king ordered that the servant and his wife and children and everything they owned be sold to pay back the debt.

The servant threw himself at the king's feet. "Have pity on me, master. Give me time, and I promise I will pay back everything in full."

The king was so touched by the servant's plea that he let him go and canceled the debt.

But as the servant went out, he came upon one of his fellow servants who owed him only one hundred denarii. Seizing him by the throat, the servant shouted, "Pay back what you owe me."

The fellow servant fell to his knees and pleaded, "Please be patient with me, and I will pay you back."

The servant refused and had his fellow servant thrown in prison.

When the other servants of the king saw this, they went to the king and told him the whole story.

The king sent for the first servant. "You wicked man," the king said. "Didn't I forgive you your whole debt to me? Why then couldn't you show the same kindness to your fellow servant?"

The king was so angry that he handed the servant over to the jailers until he could pay all his debt.

God will do the same to you if you do not forgive each other from the heart.

The Laborers in the Vineyard

Once there was a landowner who went out very early in the morning to hire laborers to work in his vineyard.

After agreeing to the usual day's pay, he sent them off to work.

Three hours later, the landowner saw some men standing idle in the marketplace.

The landowner said, "Go and join the others in the vineyard, and I promise to pay you a fair wage." So off they went.

Around midday, the landowner made the same arrangement with more men standing around. At three in the afternoon, he did the same thing.

An hour before sunset, the landowner went out and again he saw some men standing idle. "Why aren't you out working?" the landowner asked.

"Because no one has hired us," the men answered. So the landowner sent them to the vineyard to work with the others.

When evening came, the landowner told his servant, "Call the laborers and pay them, beginning with the ones who came last and ending with those who came first."

The men who had begun working one hour before sunset came and were paid a full day's wage.

When it was time to pay the laborers who had been hired first, they expected to be paid extra, but they were paid the same amount as all the others.

They began to grumble.

"These latecomers have only worked an hour, yet you paid them the same as us who have stood and sweated in the hot sun all day long."

The landowner turned and said to one of them, "My friend, I'm not being unfair to you. You agreed to the usual wage, didn't you? Take it and go home.

"Surely I am free to pay the last man the same as you. Do not be angry if I choose to be generous."

So the last will be first and the first last.

The Prodigal Son

There was a man with two sons, and the younger one said to his father, "Father, I would like my share of the property. Will you give it to me?" So the father divided the estate between the two sons.

Shortly after, the younger son turned his share into cash and went off to a distant land where he soon spent it all in wild and reckless living.

A severe famine came upon the land and the young man was in desperate need.

So, he went and attached himself to a local landowner who sent him into the fields to tend pigs.

The young man would have gladly eaten the husks that the pigs were eating, as no one gave him anything to eat.

But suddenly, he came to his senses. "My father has hired servants that have more than enough to eat, and here I am starving to death.

"I will go back home to my father and say to him, 'Father, I have sinned against God and against you.

'I'm no longer worthy to be called your son. Treat me as one of your paid servants.'"

So, he started for home, to his father's house. While he was still a ways off, his father saw him coming and was so happy that he ran to meet him. He threw his arms around his son and kissed him.

The young man said, "Father, I have sinned against God and against you. I'm no longer worthy to be called your son."

But the father called his servants and said, "Quickly, fetch the best robe and put it on my son. Put rings on his fingers and shoes on his feet.

"Bring the fatted calf and kill it, for we will have a feast today.

"My son was dead and has come back to life. He was lost and is now found." And the celebration began.

Now, the older son had been out in the fields and as he came near the house, he heard the sound of music and dancing.

He called to one of the servants and asked what was going on.

The servant answered, "Your brother has come home, and your father has killed the fatted calf because he is safe and sound. There is a celebration."

The older brother was angry and refused to go in to the party. The father came out and pleaded with the young man to join the celebration.

"I have slaved for you all these years," the older brother said. "I have never disobeyed you, yet you have never even given me a baby goat for a feast with my friends.

"But my brother comes home after spending all his money on wild and reckless living, and you kill the fatted calf for him."

"My son," the father said, "you are always with me and everything I have is yours.

"But how could we help but celebrate this happy day, for your brother was dead and is now alive. He was lost and now at last is found."

The Wise and the Foolish Virgins

Once there were ten virgins who took their lamps and went out to meet the bridegroom.

Five of the maidens were wise and five of the maidens were foolish.

The foolish maidens took their lamps but did not bring any extra oil with them.

The wise maidens brought flasks of oil along with their lamps.

Now it happened that the bridegroom was late in coming, so the maidens sat down to wait, and they fell asleep.

At midnight, a cry was heard. "Behold, the bridegroom. Come out to meet him."

The maidens got up and trimmed their lamps.

The five foolish maidens said, "Oh, the flames of our lamps are dying. We are running out of oil." They said to the five wise maidens, "Give us some of your oil."

The wise maidens said, "No, there is not enough for all of us. You had better go and buy some more oil for yourselves."

And away the five foolish maidens ran. But, while they were gone, the bridegroom arrived and the five wise maidens were ready. And they went in with him to the wedding feast and the door was shut.

The five foolish maidens came back and found the door to the wedding feast closed. "My lord," they cried, "open the door to us."

But he replied, "Truly, I do not know you."

Keep awake, therefore, for you know neither the day nor the hour when the Son of Man comes.

The Great Feast

There was a king who prepared a wedding feast for his son, but when he sent his servant to gather the guests that he had invited, they all refused to come.

Each one had an excuse. One said, "I have bought a piece of land, and I must go and look it over. Please give the king my apologies."

Another said, "I've just bought five yoke of oxen, and I want to try them out. Please tell the king I am sorry."

And a third said, "I have just gotten married. Tell the king I cannot come."

The servant returned and told his master, and the king was angry. "Go out quickly," said the king, "into the streets and alleyways and bring in the poor, the crippled, the blind and the lame."

The servant said, "We have done as you ordered, master, but there is still room at the feast."

The king replied, "Go out to the highways and along the sides of the road and make the people there come in. I want my house to be full, but I'll tell you this. Not one of those who were invited shall taste my feast!"

The Pharisee and the Publican

Two men went up to the temple to pray. One was a Pharisee, the other was a tax-gatherer.

The Pharisee stood up and prayed like this: "O God, I thank thee, that I am not like the rest of men, greedy and dishonest, and especially not like this tax-gatherer here.

"I fast twice a week, and I give away a portion of all I have."

The tax-gatherer kept his distance and did not even raise his eyes to heaven. He beat his breast and said, "O God, have mercy on me. I am such a sinner."

It was the tax-gatherer who went home, forgiven for his sins. For those who exalt themselves shall be humbled, but those who humble themselves shall be exalted.